**Our Earth**

MOUNTAINS

Terry Jennings

Belitha Press

First published in Great Britain in 1999 by
Belitha Press Limited,
London House, Great Eastern Wharf,
Parkgate Road, London SW11 4NQ

Editor Honor Head
Designer Helen James
Illustrator Graham Rosewarne
Picture researcher Diana Morris

ISBN 1 85561 881 8

Printed in Hong Kong

British Library Cataloguing in Publication Data
CIP data for this book is available from the British Library

Photographic credits

Bruce Coleman Ltd: 7b G. Cubitt, 12t **Werner Stoy**, 15 **Steven Kaufman**, 17b **Geoff Dore**, 21t **Guido Gozzi**, 27t **Keith Gunnar**. **James Davis Travel Photography**: 4t. **Eye Ubiquitous**: 29t **Bob Battersby**. **FLPA**: 18b **David Hosking**, 26 W. **Wisniewski. Getty Images:** front cover, H. Richard Johnston. **GSF**: 14. **Robert Harding Picture Library**: 10b **Roy Rainford**, 12b **R. Frerck**, title page and 18t **B. Schuster**, 21b **Explorer**, 23b. **Terry Jennings**: 16, 22. **Mountain Camera/ John Cleare**: 4b, 9, 17t. **NHPA**: 25t **Robert Thompson**, 25b **R. Shaw**, 29b **David Middleton. Spectrum Colour Library**: 23c. **SPL**: 8 **Martin Bond**, 10t **David Parker. Trip**: 11 R. **Daniell. Zefa**: 5, 13, 27b.

Cover Mount Hood, Oregon, United States

Words in **bold** appear in the glossary on pages 30 and 31.

Contents

What are mountains?

Mountains and hills are high points that rise above the surrounding land. There are mountains in most countries of the world. There are even mountains under the sea. Hills are lower than mountains.

▲ *Mount Taranaki is a **volcanic** mountain in New Zealand.*

▲ *The longest mountain range is the Andes in South America.*

Mountain ranges

A few mountains, such as Fujiyama in Japan, stand alone. But most mountains are grouped together in long chains or **ranges**.

Old and new mountains

Some mountains are hundreds of millions of years old. Others are much younger and some are still forming. This book looks at how mountains begin, how they grow and how they change. It also looks at the animals, plants and people who live on mountains.

▲ *Ayers Rock in Australia was once much higher, but has been worn away.*

How mountains begin

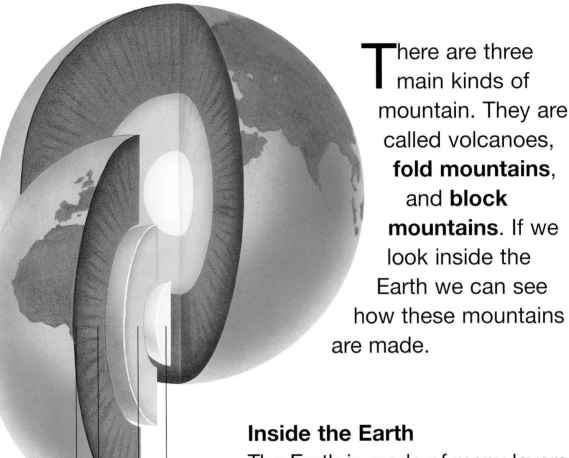

crust

mantle

outer core

inner core

▲ *The Earth is made up of layers, like a giant onion.*

There are three main kinds of mountain. They are called volcanoes, **fold mountains**, and **block mountains**. If we look inside the Earth we can see how these mountains are made.

Inside the Earth

The Earth is made of many layers. The layer we stand on is called the Earth's **crust**. Underneath the crust is the mantle which is made of rock. This rock is so hot it has melted. The **core** in the middle of the Earth is in two parts. Both parts are made of extremely hot metal.

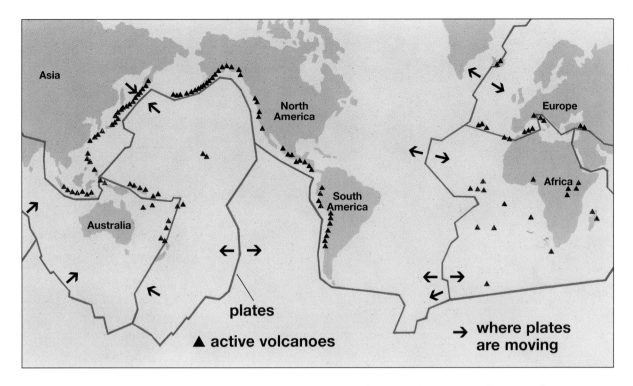

On the map:
- Asia
- North America
- Europe
- Africa
- South America
- Australia
- plates
- ▲ active volcanoes
- → where plates are moving

Pushing up

The Earth's crust is made up of huge pieces called **plates** which float on the mantle. Sometimes the plates bump into each other. When this happens, the rocks along the edges are pushed up to make mountains or hills. The Earth's crust can also be squeezed up between huge cracks in the surface to make hills and mountains.

▲ *Most volcanoes form where two plates meet or come apart.*

▼ *Smoke rises from a volcano in Indonesia.*

Fold mountains

▲ *These rocks in Dorset, England, are giant folds of the Earth's crust that have been pushed up from the sea bed.*

The world's great mountain ranges, such as the Alps, the Himalayas and the Rocky Mountains, are fold mountains.

Pushing plates

The Earth's crust is made up of layers of rock. When two of the Earth's plates push against each other, the layers of rock are pushed up into huge folds. These make long rows of mountains. The highest mountains are in the middle and there are smaller mountains on either side and rows of hills beyond.

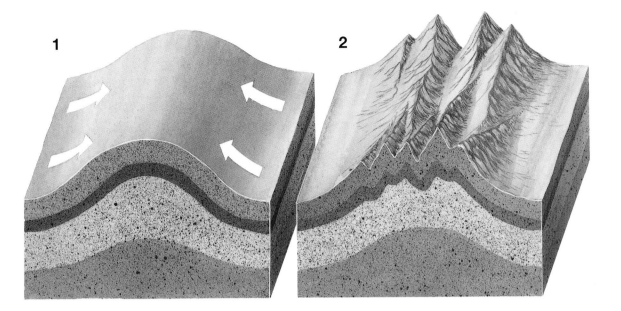

The Himalayas

The highest mountains in the world are the Himalayas. They were formed about 50 million years ago when the plate carrying India pushed into the plate carrying Asia. The flat layers of rock under the sea were squeezed and crumpled between the plates. The rocks were forced up out of the sea into giant folds. The highest mountain in the world, Mount Everest, is part of the Himalayas.

▲ *1 Layers of rock are squeezed, forming folds. 2 The rocks crack and wear away, forming mountains.*

▲ *The Himalayas is a huge mountain range in Asia.*

Block mountains

Block mountains were formed during enormous **earthquakes**. Earthquakes are caused when rocks suddenly slip. This usually happens along a huge crack or **fault**.

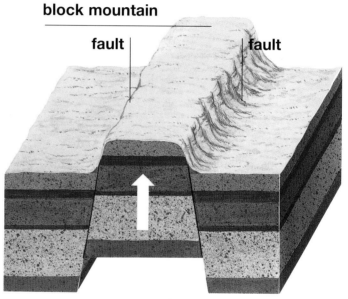

block mountain

fault   fault

▲ *The San Andreas Fault runs along the western side of the United States.*

▲ *A block mountain forms when rock is squeezed up between two faults.*

◄ *Benbulben in Ireland is a block mountain.*

Block mountains

Sometimes when two faults are fairly close to each other, great blocks of rock are squeezed up between them. These blocks of rock may form flat-topped mountains, called block mountains.

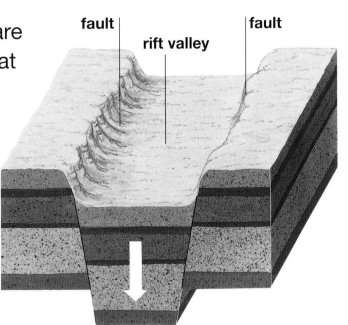

Rift valleys

Sometimes a huge slab of land slips down between two faults. It forms a wide **valley** with a flat bottom. This is called a rift valley. The biggest rift valley in the world stretches along the eastern side of Africa.

▲ *A rift valley forms when land slips down between two faults.*

▼ *The Great Rift Valley of East Africa.*

Volcanoes

Some of the world's highest mountains are volcanoes. A volcano is made of **lava**. This hot, runny rock comes from deep inside the Earth.

Active volcanoes

There are about 1300 **active** volcanoes on land in the world today. Many more are under the sea. Active volcanoes are those that erupt. When a volcano **erupts**, hot lava comes to the top and spills down the sides like a river of fire. This happens when there is a gap between the Earth's plates.

▲ *Red-hot lava flows down the sides of an active volcano.*

▶ *Mount Paricutin in Mexico was once an active volcano.*

Sleeping volcanoes

A volcano that hasn't erupted for a long time is called sleeping or **dormant**. A volcano that has been dormant may suddenly erupt again. A volcano that hasn't erupted for thousands of years is called **extinct**.

▲ *This rock in the United States is lava that hardened inside a volcano. The softer rock outside the volcano has worn away.*

► *When lava is thick, it slowly builds up a cone-shaped mountain.*

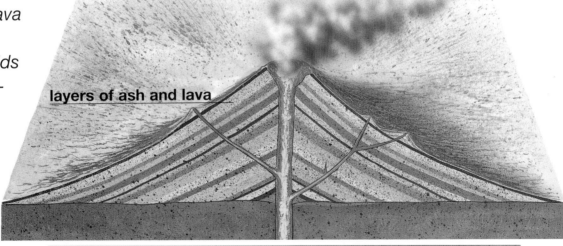

layers of ash and lava

► *When lava is thin it forms a volcano which looks like a low hill.*

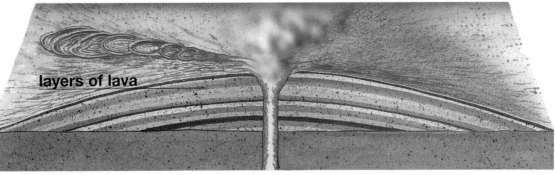

layers of lava

Mountains under the sea

▲ *Lava and hot water rise from a volcano under the sea.*

There are mountain ranges on the bottom of the sea. Most of these mountains are volcanoes.

A new volcano

Volcanoes under the sea are made from lava, like land ones. The lava rises through cracks in the Earth's crust and cools into hard layers. Each time the volcano erupts it becomes bigger.

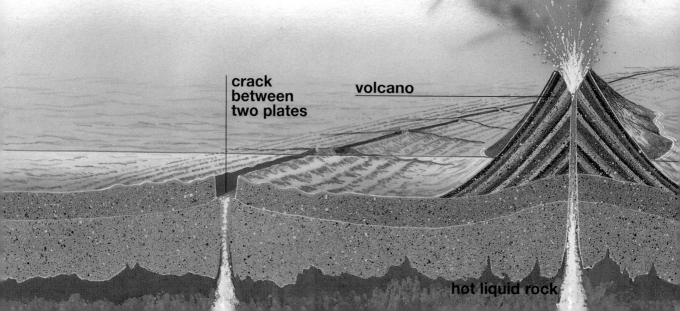

crack between two plates

volcano

hot liquid rock

▶ *The volcano Mount Augustin in Alaska erupts out of the sea. One day it may form a new island.*

Out of the ocean

Volcanoes under the sea can grow to be as big as mountains on land. Some volcanoes are so big they rise out of the sea.

A new island

When a volcano rises out of the sea, it becomes a new island. Many thousands of people live on some of these volcanic islands.

▼ *As the Earth's plates move, lava rises from cracks between them and forms volcanoes.*

sea level

Earth's crust

Wearing away

Mountains are getting smaller all the time. They are worn away by wind, water, ice and chemicals.

▲ *Young mountains, like the European Alps, are high and jagged.*

The power of ice

Water runs into the cracks in rocks. When it freezes, the ice presses against the sides of each crack. Pieces of rock break off and fall down the mountain.

▼ *Rain and ice cause bits of rock to come loose from the mountain.*

freezing water splits rock

small pieces of rock

large pieces of rock roll furthest

◄ *Old mountains, like Ben Nevis in Scotland, have rounded peaks.*

▼ *When rainwater slowly rots away limestone, it makes a limestone pavement.*

Heat and cold

In deserts, the hot days and cold nights slowly weaken rocks until pieces break off. Chemicals in rainwater can slowly rot away some rocks, such as **limestone**.

Worn away

All this wearing away of rocks, by sun, rain, ice and snow, is called weathering. Plants also wear away rocks. Their roots grow into cracks and break up the rocks.

Water power

Rivers help to wear away mountains and to change the shape of a mountain. They move loose rocks to other places.

Rivers at work

Stones broken from mountains are washed along by rivers and streams. These stones rub against each other and slowly break down into gravel and mud.

▲ *A young mountain stream can move stones and big boulders.*

▼ *A gentle river can form a flat valley.*

Soft and hard rocks

Rivers wear away soft rocks more easily than harder rocks. Where hard rock lies on top of soft rock, the hard rock is often left behind as a ledge. Then the river pours over it in a **waterfall**.

New land

After thousands of years, rivers and **streams** wear down mountains into hills and valleys. The sand, gravel and mud which have been worn off the mountains are carried down towards the sea. Here they may form new land.

rain falls on mountains

loose bits of rock

waterfall

river bank

▶ *Rivers and streams drop loose bits of rock from the mountains along the river banks to form new land.*

Rivers of ice

▼ *A glacier starts when snow piles up in the hollows on a mountain. The snow turns to ice which slides down the mountain.*

High in the mountains where it is very cold, there are rivers of ice, called **glaciers**. These are made when snow falls and settles. As the snow piles up, it turns to ice. Eventually, the thick layer of ice slides slowly down the mountain.

On the move

As the glacier moves down the mountain, it picks up pieces of rock. These scrape against the mountain as they move. Over thousands of years, the glacier cuts a valley in the mountain.

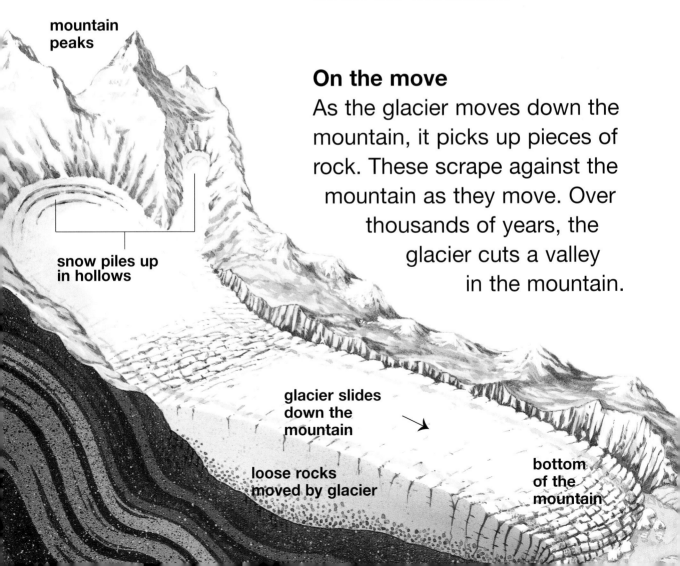

mountain peaks

snow piles up in hollows

glacier slides down the mountain

loose rocks moved by glacier

bottom of the mountain

◄ A valley made by a glacier in the Ordesa National Park in Spain.

New valleys

We can't see the valleys made by glaciers until the ice melts. When this happens the water flows out from the end of the glacier as a river. This river also wears away the mountain rock. There are valleys all over the world that have been shaped by glaciers that have now melted.

▲ A glacier will flow as long as new ice forms in the mountains.

Wet and dry

T he higher you go up a mountain, the colder and windier it gets. There is always snow on top of high mountains.

▲ *Many mountains are so high they are always covered in snow, even those in hot countries.*

Rising clouds

Clouds form over the water and the wind blows them up the mountain side. As the clouds rise over the mountains they cool and it rains.

▼ *As clouds rise above the mountain they cool down and it rains.*

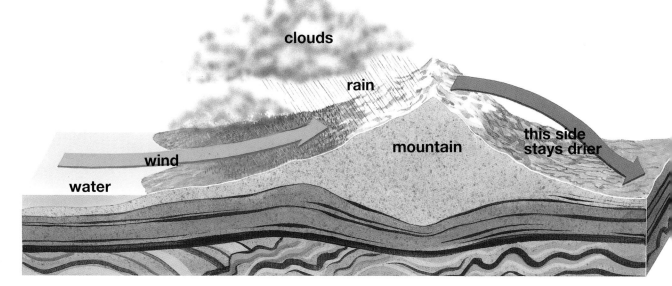

clouds

rain

mountain

this side stays drier

wind

water

The wet side

The side of a mountain where the wind blows is often very wet because it rains a lot. The other side, where the wind doesn't blow, has very little rain and is much drier.

The Rockies

The Rocky Mountains of North America have a wet side and a dry side. The west coast of America has plenty of rain. But the eastern side of the mountains is hot, dry desert.

▼ *The eastern side of the Rocky Mountains is a burning hot desert.*

▲ *The western side of the Rocky Mountains has a lot of rain and is very green and fertile.*

Plants and wildlife

Mountains are difficult places for plants and animals to live. It is windy and there is not much soil. There may be snow on the ground for months.

The tree-line

There are often forests on the lower slopes of mountains. Above a certain height, called the **tree-line**, it is too cold and windy for trees to live.

◄ *The plants change as you go up a mountain.*

alpine plants

pasture

tree-line

forests

Mountain plants

High in the mountains there are often areas of grass or pasture. Higher still, small plants, called **alpine plants**, grow. They have long roots to hold them in place when the strong winds blow. Alpine plants have bright flowers to attract the few insects which live this high up.

▲ *Alpine **pastures** are covered with wild flowers in the summer.*

▲ *Rocky Mountain goats have thick coats to keep them warm.*

Mountain animals

Many animals live in the mountains. They often have thick coats to keep them warm. Some animals, such as ground squirrels and bears, sleep, or hibernate, through the winter. Others, such as mountain hares and stoats, turn white so that they are **camouflaged** against the snow.

Living on mountains

Only a few people live high up on mountains. Many more people live and work on the lower slopes and in the valleys where the weather is warmer.

▼ *Grape vines growing on the lower slopes of a mountain in Germany.*

Alpine pastures

In the European Alps, farmers keep their **cattle** in sheds in the valleys during the winter. In the summer, they take the cattle up to the high pastures above the tree-line to feed. Some of the farmers live in small houses high in the mountains during the summer so they can be near their cattle.

Mountain crops

People grow crops such as tea, potatoes and fruit trees on the lower slopes of some mountains.

Minerals and wood

Many useful **minerals** come from mountain rocks. Some people who live on or near mountains dig up these minerals. They mine coal, iron, copper, silver and gold. Other people work in the forests, cutting down the trees for timber and paper.

▲ *Many people visit mountains to ski, walk and climb.*

◄ *A large copper mine has been dug in this mountain in Utah in the United States.*

Fragile mountains

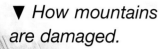

▼ *How mountains are damaged.*

rain

too many walkers wear away plants

too many animals eat the plants

The weather is slowly wearing away mountains. But in some places people and their animals are also damaging mountains.

Washed away

If too many sheep, goats or other animals eat the mountain plants, or if too many trees are cut down, the rain washes away the soil. When this happens no more plants can grow on the mountain side.

too many trees are cut down

soil is washed away

soil blocks rivers and streams

▲ *Many thousands of people visit some of the world's highest mountains.*

National parks

Many mountain areas which attract lots of people are now national parks. National parks are areas of land where the natural beauty and wildlife are protected.

Fragile mountains

Although they look very strong, mountains are really fragile. If we take care of our mountains they will last for many more years.

Damage by tourists

If too many people walk up a mountain path they kill the plants growing on it. When it rains, water rushes down the path and washes away the soil and rocks.

▲ *Walkers in Yosemite National Park, California, United States.*

Glossary

active (of a volcano) A volcano that erupts from time to time.

alpine plants Small plants, usually with brightly coloured flowers, which live on high mountains.

block mountains Flat-topped mountains formed when a large block of land is pushed up between two faults.

camouflage The way an animal blends in with its surroundings. This makes it difficult to see so that it is hidden from other animals.

cattle Cows and bulls.

core The centre of the Earth.

crust The Earth's outer layer of rock on which we live.

dormant (of a volcano) Resting or inactive, not erupting.

earthquake A violent shaking of the ground when the Earth's plates move.

erupt (of a volcano) When hot lava pours from the top of a volcano and spills down the sides.

extinct (of a volcano) No longer active or erupting.

fold mountains Mountains pushed up into huge folds or ridges by movements of the Earth's plates.

fault A large crack or break in a series of rocks.

glacier A river of ice which flows down a mountain.

lava The hot, runny rock that comes out of a volcano.

limestone Soft, grey rock.

mineral Any useful material found in the Earth which does not come from plants or animals.

pasture The grassy land where cattle feed.

plates The large pieces that make up the Earth's crust. The slow, steady movements of the plates cause the changes in the shape of the Earth's surface.

range A row or line of mountains.

stream The early stage of a river. A stream often starts high up in the mountains and has fast-flowing water.

tree-line The point on a mountain where trees can grow. Above the tree-line it is too cold or windy for trees to live.

valley A stretch of lower land between hills or mountains.

volcano A mountain which pours out lava.

waterfall A fall of water where a river or stream flows over a cliff or large rock.

Index

bold = a picture reference